Be Happy Now

Other Titles by Annie Jean Brewer:

Nonfiction Titles:
The Shoestring Girl: How I Live on Practically
      Nothing...And YOU Can Too!
The Minimalist Cleaning Method
400 Ways to Save a Fortune
How to Watch Movies and Television Shows for Free
How to Write and Sell an Ebook
How to Write Ebooks For a Living
Where to Work Online
Professional Help: How to Prevent and Fix Malware,
      Viruses, Spyware and Other Baddies
How to Watch Stuff Online For Free
Be Happy Now
How to Be Happy

Fiction Titles:
163 Nights
The Bean Pot and Other Tales
What About Bob?

Be Happy Now

Annie Jean Brewer

Table of Contents

Be Happy

There is a lot of focus on the negative in this world. It can be seriously overwhelming, especially in the light of our own problems. Seriously, when people call and visit, what do most of them like to talk about? Negative things, which add to the other negative things in your life, and drag you even lower than you were to begin with!

Change will not come into your life until you change yourself. Everything you think, everything you feel is essentially a wish you have placed on the winds of the Universe. *Everything*. No exceptions. Those feelings we feel are wishes as well, stronger wishes than spoken words, written words and even visualization. Change those feelings and you change yourself.

Being happy now is the secret to changing your world and reality. It changes your focus, clearing your mind and enabling yourself to see opportunities that have been there all along but were invisible to you. Being happy now will give you the energy to pounce upon those opportunities when they appear and the ability to know that you are heading toward your goal.

When the roof leaks, the bills are overdue, the spouse is cheating or life just sucks, finding that happiness can seem impossible. When you are lying in your bed wanting to die you may think that finding happiness is a stupid goal, that things have to change to make the happiness come. That couldn't be farther from the truth.

The Happiness Snowball

When I first started looking for things to be happy about, all I could find was bedtime. I was so happy that the day was over and I could relax in my bed with no one to bother me. Each night when I would go to bed I would thank the Universe for bedtime; for the comfy clean sheets, the soft warm blankets, the pillow that fit my head *"just so;"* soon I realized that life was incredibly peaceful in the mornings when I first awoke, and I would stretch and turn and snuggle down again, thanking the Universe for the peaceful snuggly blankets and yet another moment of calm in my day.

That happiness snowball got a little bigger as I realized just how lucky I was to be able to take a hot bath every day, and I reminded myself of the days when I would have to go to friend's houses just to take a shower. I would lie in the bathtub reveling in the heat and moist environment, thanking the Universe for such a perfect bath!

Then I would see the little animals outside my window, or pass them as I was driving by and see the beauty and majesty within them and say a little word of gratitude for being a witness to their beauty.

The happier I became, the more my life started to change. I was led to read books on self-improvement, to start seeking how to be better and improve my life. Soon a total stranger was pressing a book called _The Secret_ into my hands and that was when my journey truly became magical.

All of this, all of who I am today came about as a result of the fact that I was tired of being miserable; I was tired of having nothing good to say about anything. I hated when folks asked how I was doing, because I would have to say something bad or keep my mouth shut. It sucked big time, and I had enough of that feeling.

Little did I know that the happier I became, the more magical life would become, as it snowballed! This happiness snowball is something we all need in our lives, but sometimes it is a challenge to find that first little thing to be happy about. Look around your house: can you enjoy a cup of coffee or tea? Perhaps a hot bath would give you pleasure? Look for one thing and focus on the joy it gives you, like the pleasure of a pet or a child.

You can start your happiness snowball rolling by making the baby steps listed in the next chapter "Exercise the Happy Muscle."

Exercise the Happy Muscle

Happiness is like any other muscle in your body; use it or lose it. Once it atrophies you have to work harder to get it back, but it is not impossible to accomplish.

Find one tiny thing in your life to be happy for, and be thankful for that one little thing.

- *Did you get to work on time?*
- *Did your child take a first step, or say a first word?*
- *Did your pet actually go outside to use the bathroom today, instead of the living room floor?*

- *Were you able to fix Ramen noodles without burning them*
- *Did you have enough money to pay a particular bill?*
- *Are you finally in bed after a long day?*

Just take a moment and say "thank you" for that one tiny thing. Take a deep breath and be happy that you paid that bill, got that hug or heard that song! You can spend your days only once, do you want to squander them on unhappiness, or create a treasure house of good memories?

Take a piece of paper and write a letter to that you hold divine. Call it the Universe, God, Jehovah, Allah—whatever name you consider your holy one, but write a letter and thank this being for the good things in your life.

Dear Jehovah,

Thank you for the little birdie that tapped on my window today! I feel bad cause I had neglected to put out any bird seed this winter, and this little guy looked me in the eye and told me he was hungry! I went right then to the store and got food for him and his friends, plus some corn for the squirrels.

The cardinals watched me scatter the seed by my windowpane and assemble the new feeder. They hardly waited until I was in the house before starting to chow down! Thank you for giving me the money to feed these little guys!

I can hear one of the squirrels on the roof as I type this—he is running toward the porch. Won't he be happy to see I have put some corn out there for him! I love feeding the little animals!

This morning I woke up on my own, without a phone ringing, an alarm going off or a noise to disturb my slumber. Thank you for letting me wake up so peacefully!

I got a call from Katie today, she wanted to sing me a song along with a video game a friend of hers has. At first I was annoyed, but then I realized that she loved me so much that she took time away from her friend to share this moment with me! Thank you so much for her love!

I have a pot of beans cooking on the stove, they smell so good! They remind me of eating at a big table with friends, platters filled with fried taters, corn bread, beans and all sorts of other goodies. I can hardly wait until they are done!

Well, I've got to get back to work on this book, Jehovah. Thank you again for helping me find what to write!

Love,

Annie

That is the letter I wrote today; I have included it to show you that you can put anything in these little notes to the Universe, and as a reminder that a gift doesn't have to be big in order to be appreciated.

Make a List

Another thing you can do is make a list. Take a blank piece of paper, and on every other line write something you are thankful for. On the empty spaces in-between put something that concerns you right now. When you are done, read over the note and be happy that all of those concerns you penciled in will be resolved and become more things to be happy for.

My Happy List

I own my car, paid-for
I want this book to help others
I own my own house, paid-for
I want ideas for more helpful books
I can feed the animals
I want a mild winter
I am happy
I want to learn how to reach more people
I am loved

Write out your happy list whenever you have something that bothers you. The lines in italic are my concerns, surrounded by the miracles that have already happened in my life. Just read the list and remind yourself that this is your happy list, that only good can come to you and everything will be okay.

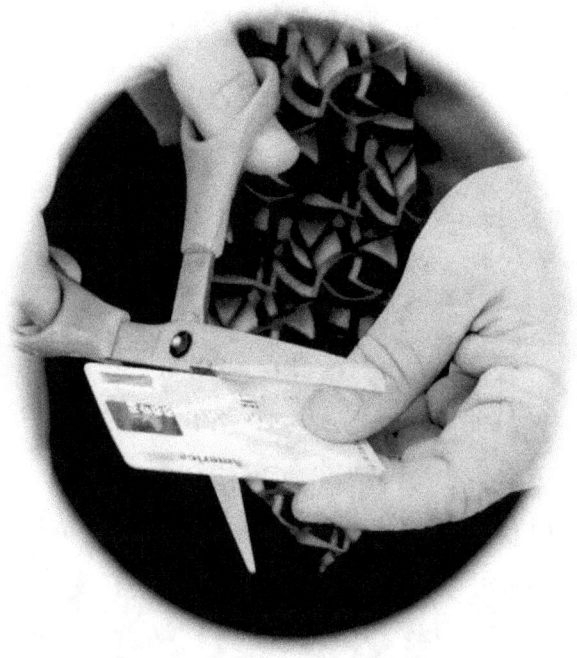

Destroy Your Problems

Another thing that can help is to destroy your problems and kick them out of your life. Here are a few ways to do this.

Scissors

Take a sheet of paper and tear it into pieces. On each piece write out something that is bothering you. It could be a bill or anything. Say you are afraid of being laid off at your job, write that down on a piece of paper and fold it over once or twice.

Take a pair of scissors and cut that problem up! Say goodbye to that problem, and tell yourself how much you enjoy cutting that problem out of your life! Heck, I've taken problems, tossed them on the ground and jumped on them a few times for good measure!

When you are done, make a big to-do about tossing that problem in the trash, but don't leave it there! Gather up the trash bag that contains it and get it out of your house! Imagine that you are getting the problem out of your house and your life as you take out that trash, and feel the joy of it finally being GONE! Whoot! Hooray! Celebrate by dancing, listening to music, just whatever allows you to continue feeling that good, happy feeling. Remember you have chopped it up and tossed it out of your life, so that problem has no more control over you!

Fire

First, find a safe spot where you can burn some little things. Sometimes I go out in my back yard, use my grill, or place a skillet on the stove with the fan on and some baking soda around. Just find a spot where you won't set the house on fire or trip the smoke alarms.

Take a piece of paper and write down your problem. Feel yourself putting that problem down on that piece of paper, then light it and watch it burn. Seeing those words turn to ash has a mystical feeling to it, for your problems are burning away, turning into smoke and ash. Sometimes this is one of my favorite ways of dealing with problems, but other times I get more enjoyment out of beating up that piece of paper before cutting it up or lighting it. If you really want it gone, write it down, stomp on it, hit it, yell at it, cut it up in teeny tiny pieces and THEN set it on fire and laugh while it fades away! Sprinkle the ashes somewhere away from your home and feel the wind carrying away the last of your issues.

Jedi Visualization

Find a spot where you can play some music and be alone. Put on some really good fight music, close your eyes and imagine your problem as some sort of monster in front of you. It can be a glowing orb, a Sith lord, a Romulan, just whatever shape your problem decides to take.

Close your eyes and reach for the saber you envision at your belt. Ignite it, and attack the problem that stands before you. Strike it down, over and over, however many times you want to. Depending upon how strong the problem has gripped you, it may fight back with weapons of its own--that's okay! Know that you are the master and it cannot win, and fight with all of your might. When you strike the death blow, watch your problem disappear before your eyes and celebrate! Dance with happiness because you have vanquished your enemy!

I have a confession to make: I've been doing that since I first read "Star Wars" as a kid. It really makes me feel better to visualize my enemies and stomp them into the ground! Course, my folks didn't understand what I was doing, but who cares? It was a great stress release, and I had no idea I was casting my problems out of my life until many years later!

By casting physical representations of your problems aside, you release the negative energy associated with them and bring positive energy into your life. This energy is a

Annie Jean Brewer

powerful force in eliminating issues and achieving dreams.

Keeping the Happy Feelings

Once your happy muscle starts working again, feed it with more happy things. Read news websites that focus on good things like the Good News Network and Happy News. When someone tries to talk about negative things, change the subject or end the conversation.

When you find yourself once again traveling down that slope of negativity, stop yourself. Sometimes the best way is to literally tell yourself "quit it!" Deliberately choose a subject that feels good to you, write a happy list or a thank-you note for something good in your life.

Negativity and happiness are habits; once you get into the habit of being negative, you have to work to change that habit. Once you do, however, your world will start to change around you!

A Gift to You

I know personally what it is like to be so down that you want to die. I've been there, to the point where I seriously considered taking my own life. It hurts to feel that you are alone and that things are not going to get any better!

Things can and will improve my friends but the first thing you have to focus on is something you can control--yourself. Focus on what you can control and watch it radiate out to other areas of your life!

I am Annienygma, and like you, I am on a journey to find myself, improve myself and make my dreams come true. It is my hope that by sharing my journeys, the things I do to make my *now* better while reaching toward my tomorrow will help others on their paths.

It is my hope that this will help many people, so please share this book with family, friends and anyone else in need of the tips I have placed within. Just stop by my site at http://annienygma.com, say hello and let me know if this has helped you any at all.

Know that you are loved, and that you are not alone. Not ever.

Love,

Annie

A Request

Please leave an honest review of this book at
the website of your choice. This will help
others like you determine if this book will help
them. To thank you for your review I will be
happy to send you a PDF copy of this book so
that you can store it on your computer, share
with friends or print it out as desired. Please
email me at annie@annienygma.com with a
link to your published review and I will send
you the PDF copy of this book.

Thank you!

Annienygma

About the Author

Annie Brewer is a frugal living expert who combines minimalism with frugality to be a stay at home single mom to her daughter. She is the author of the popular book <u>The Shoestring Girl: How I Live on Practically Nothing And YOU Can Too!</u>, <u>The Minimalist Cleaning Method Expanded Edition</u> and a number of other titles. You can learn more about her at Annienygma.com. She has written several books on a variety of subjects, they are featured on her website and at a book retailer near you.

She currently lives in Central Kentucky with her teenage daughter and a small menagerie of pets.

Connect With Annie Online:

Main Website:
http://annienygma.com

Email:
annie@annienygma.com

Amazon Author Page:
http://www.amazon.com/author/annienygma

Facebook:
http://www.facebook.com/annienygma

Twitter:
http://www.twitter.com/annienygma

Yahoo! Contributor Network:
http://contributor.yahoo.com/user/annienygma

Smashwords:
http://www.smashwords.com/profile/view/annienyg
ma

For further information read
How to Be Happy by Annie Jean Brewer

THE
SHOESTRING
GIRL

How I Live on
Practically Nothing...
And YOU Can Too!

ANNIE BREWER

Do You Want to Live on Less?

Would you like to learn how from someone who actually does?

Over ten years ago I found myself a single mother with three children to raise.

I had to learn fast.

I had to support those kids on a fast food paycheck while I put myself through school.

Not only did I manage to do it but I topped my own expectations. We ended up living better than I <u>ever</u> would have imagined.

Since then I have not only quit my day job but I have built up sufficient income to become a single stay-at-home mother to my youngest child. This feat would not have been possible without the frugality of shoestring living.

We live well on about $500 a month - and know how to live on even LESS!

Over the years I have shared my secrets with others who have fallen on hard times. I have helped friends who became disabled, single parents, the unemployed and others who found a need to live on as little money as possible.

The first thing I always shared was the timeless words of my grandmother. Even now I can hear her reminding me to hold up my head because...

"There's no sin in being poor!"

This may be your first brush with life below the poverty line. You may be scared. You may be ashamed. You may not know what to do or where to start.

I'm here to help you save money

I have drawn upon my 10+ years of personal experience to create the ultimate frugal living guide. I won't bore you with stupid fluff about clipping coupons. Instead, you will find a concise method you can implement to save thousands of dollars over the course of a year.

Sections Include:
Housing
Auto
Groceries (Includes raising food)
Computers (includes where to find free and inexpensive software)
Television (includes watching shows online for free)
Books (lots of links to free ebooks and how to search for free ebooks online)
Music (includes links for free music sites)
Clothing
Cleaning tips and recipes
Personal care tips and recipes
Furniture
Thrift Shops
Yard Sales

Jobs and self-employment
And much more!

I not only explain the exact methods that I use to save money and live frugally but I also explain how I could live on about <u>half</u> of the money that I actually do.

While you may not wish to apply everything here I am confident that you will be inspired to save more money than you ever thought possible. You will learn the skills you need to overcome your current financial challenge.

Start Saving Money Today!

Available in both print and ebook format at many popular retailers.

HOW TO
WRITE EBOOKS
FOR A LIVING

By

Annie Brewer

Do you Want to Earn a Living from Ebooks?

As a single mother I asked the question: *How can I stay at home with my child but still pay the bills?*

Job after job kept taking me away from my daughter's fleeting childhood. My frustration grew every time I missed another milestone in her life.

I combed the Internet in search of the answer. I found several places online where you could work from home but many of these kept me literally chained to a computer for hours on end. There had to be a better way!

One day I stumbled upon a blogger selling ebooks from his website. Not only selling them, he was actually earning his living from ebook sales!

"I can do that!" I thought.

I contacted him, buttered him up and picked his brain.

Gleefully following his instructions I finished my first ebook, published it online and drooled at the screen in anticipation.

I sat, I watched, I waited. After my first few sales the money dried up like a puddle in the desert.

What was I doing wrong?

I went out in search of more writers and picked a few more brains. I stayed up late at night researching and experimenting, determined to become a successful ebook writer. I refused to give up and quit.

I discovered the secret to ebook success.

Now I spend my days at home instead of at the dreaded day job. I take long walks with my daughter instead of punching a time clock. Money comes automatically now so I can relax and enjoy my life.

Anyone can make a living with ebooks, GUARANTEED

If you follow the steps in this guide you are **guaranteed** to earn money with ebooks. I am so convinced that you will be able to earn a living entirely from ebook sales that I offer you a **6-month money-back guarantee.** If after 6 months of applying this method you are not earning money from your ebooks send me a copy of your purchase receipt and I will refund your purchase price.

This guide teaches you:
- What equipment you need to write ebooks
- What bank accounts you need
- How to financially prepare to live off your ebook royalty income
- Where to find the time to write
- The importance of a blog
- Where to practice writing in preparation
- Where to find subjects to write about
- How to create your ebook
- Where and how to create an ebook cover
- Ebook descriptions
- Where to distribute your ebook
- Ebook pricing
- The importance of a backlist
- Social media
- Making the leap by quitting your day job
- ***And more!***

"A journey of a thousand miles begins with a single step." - Confucius.

Will you take that step today?

Where to
Work Online

By
Annie Jean Brewer

Do you want to work at home?

There are so many scams out there it is hard to determine legitimate work at home jobs. It took me years of searching and I stumbled upon my first legitimate opportunity entirely by chance.

Since then I have learned how to work entirely from home and have compiled a list of legitimate work at home opportunities. There is a little here for everyone as well as tips to avoid getting ripped off by the scams out there.

This book shows you:

- The Golden Rule to working online
- Money Matters
- Multiple Income Streams
- Fast Cash
- Tinkering Cash
- Searching Cash
- Writing Cash
- Therapy Cash
- Affiliate Links
- Roll Your Own (ebook that is..)
- Phone Actresses
- "Official" Jobs
- Clearinghouses
- The Big List of Online Jobs
- *And more!*

If you are serious about working online, this is the only book you need.

400 WAYS TO SAVE A FORTUNE

ANNIE BREWER

"He that can live sparingly need not be rich."
Benjamin Franklin

There are a lot of frugality books out there.

I know. I've bought most of them.

Saving money isn't just a hobby for me; it is a way of life. It is what allows me to be a single stay-at-home mother for my child. We currently live on about $500 a month but if we wanted to we could easily live on **less.**

Here are just a few of the tips that I personally use to save thousands of dollars a year:

Tip #1 - Auto purchases. Annual Savings: $5,364.
Tip #32 - General Cleaning. Annual Savings: $216.
Tip #45 - Carpet cleaning. Annual Savings: $100.
Tip #67 - Salvaging stained clothing. Annual Savings: $50.
Tip #78 - Printer ink. Annual Savings: $100.
Tip #89 - Software. Annual Savings: $200
Tip #95 - Movies. Annual Savings: $52
Tip #100 - Television. Annual Savings: $1,200
Tip #114 - Credit Cards. Annual Savings: $480
Tip #129 - Where to work for Maximum savings. Annual savings: $1,011
Tip #241 - Housing. Annual Savings: $3,600

What could you do with that much extra money?

Written by the author of <u>The Shoestring Girl: How I Live on Practically Nothing and You Can Too</u>, this guide covers:

- Auto
- Cleaning
- Computers
- Entertainment
- Finance
- Food
- Gardening
- General Household
- Housing
- Kids
- Personal Care
- Pets
- Shopping
- Travel
- Utilities
- Funeral expenses
- *And more*

Minus the fluff, this nitty-gritty guide immediately gets down to the business of saving money with *over 400 unique tips* designed to help anyone with a desire to save money.

You may not choose to use all of the frugal ideas in this guide but I am confident that this book will inspire you to **save more money** than you ever thought possible.

How Much Can YOU save?

How to Watch Stuff Online

Annie Brewer

Annie has not paid for a cable subscription in over a decade. Instead her family watches videos online for free. In this book she shares her tips, tricks and online wisdom to teach others how they can do the same.

This book covers:
• How to protect your computer before you start
• What software you need
• A list of video websites
• How to search for more websites
• What to do when your favorite site disappears
• Video viewing tips
• How to deal with Popups and other ads
• How to buffer videos
• How to manually cache videos
• Website registration cautions
• Why not to pay for using these sites
• Torrents
• File Sharing programs
• *And more!*

Readers will not only have a resource of links to get started with but will learn how to discover even more viewing opportunities online and how to maximize their video experience while saving money in the process.

CONGRATULATIONS YOU HAVE REACHED THE END!
Thank you for your support!

***

Please help others—share this book.

www.ingramcontent.com/pod-product-compliance
Lightning Source LLC
Chambersburg PA
CBHW060006300526
45794CB00003B/1116

* 9 7 8 1 4 8 0 1 2 4 7 6 9 *